How to control cost for IT services - Startup Company

Managing cost control for IT Startup Company

Author: Shanthi Vemulapalli

Version 2.0

In my 25 plus years global experience, I have seen many startups globally [wherever I worked] they used to struggle for managing the company and the business. They also never concentrated on the required financial processes. They used to spend more time on waiting for customer appointments, meetings and engagements. They used to maintain different skill sets of the resources by paying full salary during non-project or non-billing period. Finally, they used to get answers from their beloved customers 'NO' for billable engagements.

I found with them by not following the required planning, processes, standards and work in hand. Due to lack of these, they used to burn their fingers and used to go in debt and fire the resources.

I have seen in many corporates during my services rendered to them and to their customers, they used to follow structured financial planning. I have not seen any losses by holding the resources under non-billability. Because, with their better planning and practices they used to manage the minimum profits expected by their corporate norms.

I also gathered the financial management practices from ITIL V3 practices of Service Strategy [SS]. I wrote two blogs on this kind of content, many hits used to happen.

Hence I felt to share this kind of knowledge best practices for the IT Services practitioners through this book. It has the talent acquisition and management practices also. It can help a lot towards the resource management purpose.

I took lot of pain to convert the chapter related contents into Graphics, where the reader can easily understand and remember for their live practices. Also created many live business related examples.

If you feel this should be helpful for others, I would request you to give your comment.

Table of Contents

Chapter One: Introduction

Many startup IT [Information Technology] services companies depends on particular customers business and keep continuous trust on their work orders. But inside the customer company what kind of cost cutting is happening may not be known completely by this company management. Hence with reference to the past orders flow belief, can make them confidence for their future Business continuity plan [BCP].

At one point of time the customer reveals their budget and suddenly the IT Company might get to know their fingers are burnt by investing in their resources for their customers under wait time or bench process for future projects. Then the ROI [Return On Investment] questions come into picture as below.

In such situations, how the IT startups need to be performed with cost control?

How they can best utilize their resources with prior budget and accounting planning?

How they can re-organize their operations and resources?

This E-Book covers some of the useful TIPS through the knowledge gained from the experienced IT Professional and the author; with some of the live examples demonstration from the global IT Services practices. Many charts have been depicted in the chapters with the live scenarios and also with the required processes along with the possible gaps.

This can also serve as a guide to the new PMO [Programme or project management office] staff or some practices would like to implement or improve the financial process steps to have better control of the company operation for ROI tracking.

Chapter Two: The need of financial management for a Startup IT

The financial management is a very dry subject to any IT technical savvy. I tried to link to the live scenarios to push you further reading in this E-Book. I feel every manager need to know these facts. This can help the managers for knowing their projects costing, invoicing process, and also to know their companies financial processes, etc. to be under cost control.

For any organization and to its management the challenging and critical activity is financial management. This is an extremely imperative area that enforces organizations to manage costing and resources cautiously to ensure their timely business objectives are achieved.

Normally, this function is owned by a senior executive and managed as a separate business function in an organization.

It is crucial to the IT service provider as overall organization as they must be involved in financial management also while identifying their needs, planning, designing budgets, executing the strategies, tracking the expenses and profits along with the talent management.

Chapter Three: Questions behind the Financial Management for IT company

When we consider the financial management to any Startup IT organization the following questions might arise under its objectives or measurement or for better management or under best practices of cost control for any small IT company:

1.	Did you define the financial framework of the organization on how to operate?

2.	Using this framework Can the service provider [IT startup or small company]; identify, manage, and communicate the actual cost of the service delivery?

3.	Does this framework helps in understanding the changed or new service or with the latest organizational strategies impact or implications?

4.	Do you have a structured plan to secure the funds during the IT services providing?

5.	Do you have defined methods on cross charging within the organization for internal services [under Operational Level Agreements (OLAs)]?

6.	Do you have automated systems to have the latest assets information [like; Asset, configuration management process, etc...] to measure their cost?

7.	Do you have any internal measurement for resourcing and their usage cost for different activities or projects along with their performance measurement?

8.	Do you have defined procedures to measure the timely profits with the help of the income and expenses?

9.	Do you have automated system with tracking mechanism on expenses measurement for any service under execution or to be executed or predicted for a customer?

10.	Do you have reporting process on timely expenses to report to stake holders?

11.	Do you have the mechanism to adopt and apply the company policies and practices related to financial controls?

12.   Do you have mechanism to understand the future financial requirements of the organization?*

13.   Do you have the mechanism for providing the financial forecasting and budgeting?

14.   Do you have the mechanism to have continual improvement in Company policies, financial frameworks, controls, practices, implementation, usage and tracking its benefits or ROI?

If most of the above questions don't denote the right answers as per the process or standards, it should come under category of lack of financial practices.

You can see the lack of Financial Management practices situation in a graphical chart below, in a Startup IT company:

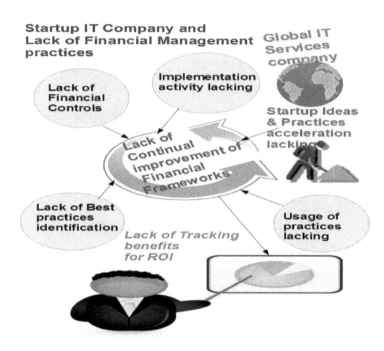

Figure 1: Startup IT Company and lack of financial management practices

Further chapters elaborate on the processes involved in financial management. Through them the best practices or solutions can be found to have pleasant financial control for IT startup business.

Chapter Four: The main processes in financial management

I would like to elaborate on the critical processes of financial management for a Startup IT company to sustain their business plans.

The financial management consists of three main processes for any kind of business organization. They are:

- Budgeting
- Accounting
- Charging

The following Figure might depict the situations through the questions on these three main processes; for a non-practitioner.

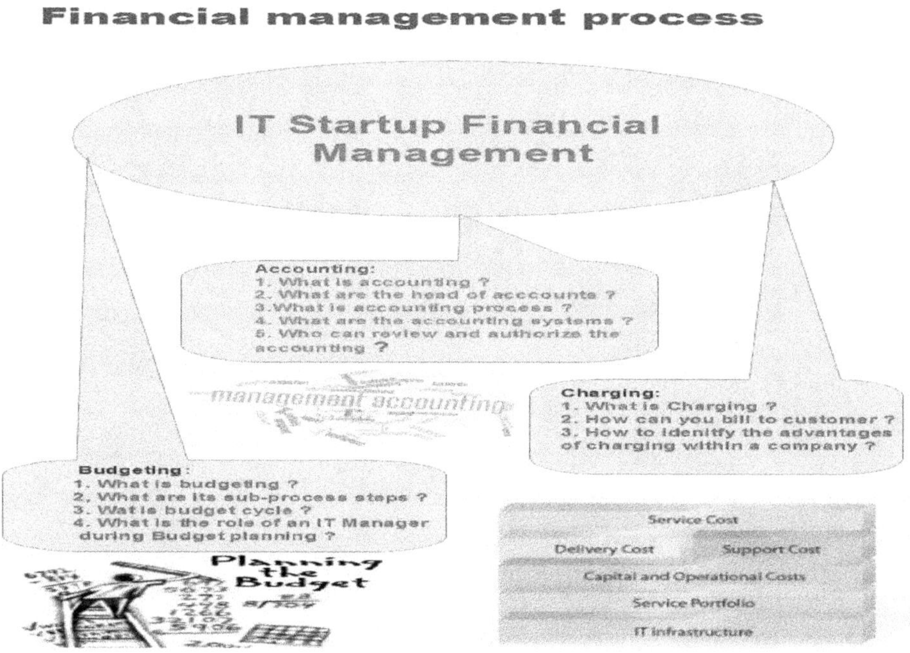

Financial management process

IT Startup Financial Management

Accounting:
1. What is accounting ?
2. What are the head of acccounts ?
3. What is accounting process ?
4. What are the accounting systems ?
5. Who can review and authorize the accounting ?

management accounting

Charging:
1. What is Charging ?
2. How can you bill to customer ?
3. How to idenitfy the advantages of charging within a company ?

Budgeting:
1. What is budgeting ?
2. What are its sub-process steps ?
3. Wat is budget cycle ?
4. What is the role of an IT Manager during Budget planning ?

Planning the Budget

Service Cost

Delivery Cost   Support Cost

Capital and Operational Costs

Service Portfolio

IT infrastructure

Figure 2: Financial management process

Now let us go through in each process phases from the above mentioned figure through the below Chapters.

Chapter Five: Budgeting in financial management

The budgeting is a process for predicting and controlling the income and expenditure of an organization. Budgeting comes under a periodic cycle. The cycle can facilitate to negotiate to set the budgets and regular or monthly monitoring of the same. The usual cycle can be yearly. On special cases it can be half year or quarterly also. If it is a startup company it is better to have a quarterly budgeting for easy tracking on ROI of different activities and to implement some of the cost controls.

The below figure can denote the typical budget assessment for IT services.

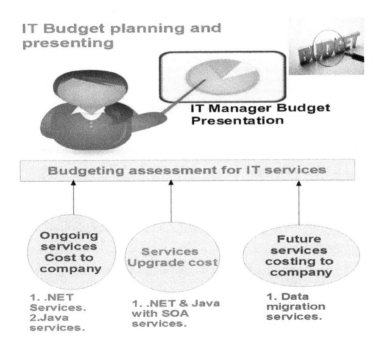

Figure 3: IT Budget planning and presenting

The below example can bring some live picture for an IT company on Budgeting action.

Example/Scenario: For any future activity, the financial planning and certain budget estimation is required. When the budgets are being developed the IT manager need to plan for ongoing costs, future costs and the upgrade cost of various services. The way the budgeting can help in identifying the differences between forecasted value and the incurred expenses value. By doing a monthly monitoring the manager can have control on the costing and expenses. The finance management team can have periodical reviews on the running cost and the predicted cost to find the ROI regularly. Even in some cases, they may not be able to get the ROI on each activity/task but monitoring helps them to estimate the predicted value.

Let us assume one payroll application need to be designed for internal use. The estimated budget can be USD 60,000 for 6 months duration. Due to the technical skills are not groomed well under ITIL V3 capacity planning process, it got delayed its implementation. The risks or measures should have been taken by comparing each month on the estimated progress and the current running progress.

The estimated plans month by month should have been there and they should have been evaluated and controlled for allocating right resources on time. Now the delay has caused the project budget increase by having some available resources and waiting for some more capable resources. The project activities for timely or right delivery might not have been synchronized.

The finance management team can track the project progress under cost measurement. At the same time there are unknown expenses can incur and those also need to be tracked. To have full cost control of any service a detailed plan might have been submitted by the IT manager and it should have been ratified by the finance team while getting approval for this kind of projects budgeting. A thorough periodical review and actions might have been implemented.

Please note due to lack of these plans and controls many IT projects have been failing and ultimately it can lead to the name of as bad resourcing also. In this case one can find the real reasons. And such plans or controls are not being enforced by either party [IT & Finance teams]; which is vulnerable to consider those projects.

The project resources also need to be educated well on these aspects under project initiation/orientation phase. When the resources are educated on these financial aspects also they feel responsible on extra or unknown costs.

Chapter Six: Accounting in financial management

Using the accounting process the IT organization can be enabled to account entirely for the way the money is spent for different activities, which is from the allocated budget. The accounting procedure should enable the cost breakdown under different heads of accounts like; customers, services, activity, resourcing or through some other aspects to assign the allocation of funds. Sometimes on each project activity also the budget can be allocated. It can be sub-divided under heads of accounts for accounting purpose.

Universally, the accounting process requires some form of accounting system like; general ledgers, journals, charts of accounts, and so on. And it should be supervised by someone with an accountancy qualification or skills. Normally a chartered accountant is qualified professional to administer these accounting procedures.

Periodical review on the allocated budget accounting is required. And also it is safe to the IT manager to have the cost control from the initiation phase of the project. This can also facilitate some buffer amount for unknown expenses. At the same time he/she can have authority to show the ROI of that project to the management.

Below figure can denote the feasible scenario for Accounting process:

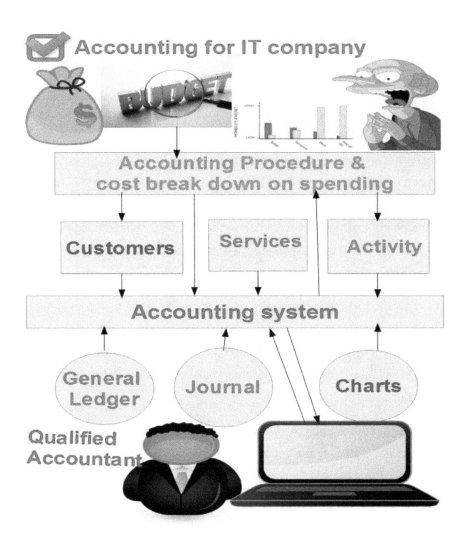

Figure 4: Accounting for IT Company

Example/Scenario:

The accounting process involves monitoring the financial management process. Like, it can involve a proper accounting of a budget. And how it is being spent or recovered, if the IT service is a charging department for their service. Let us assume, a new server setup has been done under new IT enterprise architecture department [EAD] expenses. The internal network team is an operational service department [under OLA], where they can charge the EAD. Initially EAD can allocate some identified budget for different heads of accounts. The accountant can review or supervise its expenses and ratify its spending in collaboration with the IT Manager.

The accountant should have a monthly breakdown of budget on a service providing. The summary should include Type of the account, approved budget, spent budget by each month, current balance. This way it can be balanced or if it is over spent a separate case justification need to be recorded and approval to be obtained to go head on the new or updated budget.

Sometimes the cost of the equipment might increase. In such cases this kind of process need to be followed. This way the accounting process can demonstrate and control the budget spending. Even the late joining or resignation of the resources also might create some unknown expenses due to several dependencies.

Chapter Seven: Charging in financial management

Using Charging process it can be billed to customers for the usage of the IT services. This will be applicable on the instances where organizational accounting model requires it to take place.

The below figure depicts the charging activities:

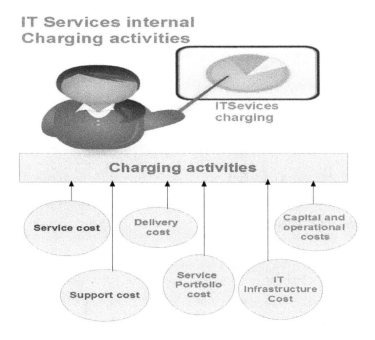

Figure 5: IT Services internal Charging activities

It definitely, requires sound accounting practices. There should be supporting systems to track the cross charging and its accuracy. We can see the examples on this process.

Example/Scenario:

In large companies most of the IT services will charge the end users and the other internal departments for the services rendered. If we consider a new employee joined in the company, this associate need to get the following:

a) Orientation training through HR,

b) Project related technical training through training division,

c) Project knowledge sharing through the team.

For a) and b) should be charged as expenses towards the new resource training to the internal business units.

Similarly, the associate might be getting a laptop and the relevant security services from ISG [Information Security Group]. It will be charged to the unit. There are many examples we can consider for internal charges depends on the company's growth and their setup.

Let us assume, a group of technical servers are being configured for customer data operations and the setup has been hosted from the Startup IT Company's [vendor] premises. Now the vendor needs to charge for this setup usage from the customer. The charges must have been denoted during the Service Level Agreements [SLAs] to the customer. This can be considered under external charging from this company to the customer.

Similarly all the expenses incurred towards the customer projects, those costs can be accounted for the business unit initially as investment and the [human and non-human] resources costing can be claimed on time. It can be like, services charges, conveyance charges, etc... later on when the invoices are being raised these should be included by the accountant for customer clarity.

All these should be there in accounting practices guidelines on how to raise a claim and the internal charges with clarity for easy operations. If the accounting procedures with more clarity or clear guidelines should have been defined and kept available for the operational staff, it can avoid confrontations within the staff and also to the customers. It is the vendor responsibility to educate the customer on this kind of company's processes in advance to the invoicing stage.

A typical setup of internal units of an IT company can be denoted from the below figure:

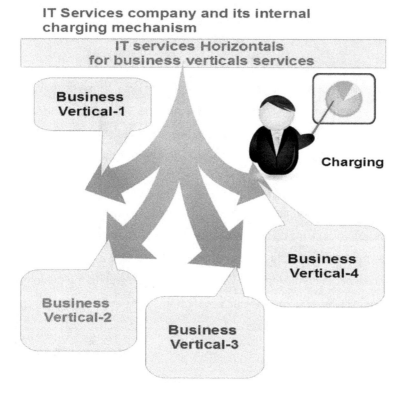

Figure 6: IT Services & Charging from Horizontals to Verticals

The advantages of the Charging:

We can identify the following advantages by having Charging methods.

- Through charging method, IT services will be able to earn revenues for internal and external operations. They can also classify their services, revenues, resources and facilities accordingly.

- The end users and departments will have options to pay and demand better services through this charging method by having the defined SLAs [for external customers] and OLAs [for internal units].

- The end users and departments can understand the better services those involve more costs.

Example: The below figure can depict some more situations:

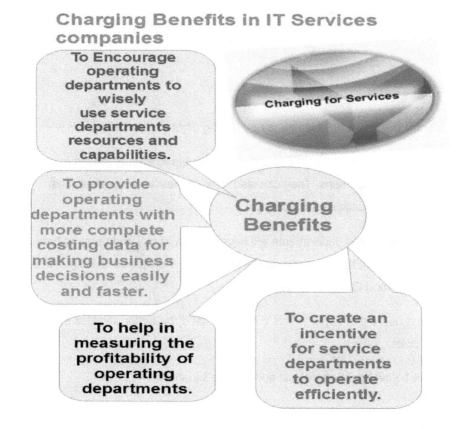

Figure 7: Charging Benefits in IT Services companies

Chapter Eight: Reporting in financial management

As we have been observing from previous definitions along with the examples/scenarios, all the financial data is business critical for a company. And all these sub-functions like, forecasting or budgeting, accounting, charging, invoicing need to be integrated for easy managing and tracking of different teams and the operations.

By using these applications any timely reports can be obtained from top management to the low level people in a company. Issues tracking can be made easy with accuracy of the calculations.

Using the financial reports, all the role based people from different departments being involved can understand them very clearly rather than with the excel sheets by having wrong and right versions.

The internal departments also can estimate their revenues for their OLAs [Operational Level Agreements]. At the same time, if the business units are having the time entry systems for resources related project work hours, the billability tracking can be made easier on weekly basis. This way the accountants also can have revenue forecasting for senior management's presentation on the company's performance.

If any customer terminates the projects within their notice period as per the SLAs, the management can predict the Profit and Loss [P & L] very easily and in advance to re-organize the operations with the staff rotation.

Example/Scenario:

Under financial reporting; we can consider a typical example of having an Enterprise Application Integration [EAI] projects setup for a customer. Let us assume this project/programme has different technical skills based resources requirements. And these all have been distributed across globe in six countries. The total resource size is more than 300 people. Now the Vendor team has received the request from the customer to bid for this project under Time and Material [T & M] billing. The customer team manages it. They only need the technical savvy's to operate the project by having daily billing.

The vendor team might have given a proposal to have a study phase on their technical setup and proposed initially few resources for different locations. They have estimated the resources and operation cost under study phase. In reality the Vendor worked out a budget for this phase of the services for the customer within their initial budget allocation. It means already the accounting practices have been started in the IT Company for tracking purpose.

Assume, now the resources have been landed at the customer premises and the accounts team need their weekly hours planned and spent details to record them for billability purpose. At this point of time if any automation system is in place the resources can enter their time entry on daily basis and the accounting team can track the work hours for their efforts billability.

Let us assume, the vendor hosted few servers for the customer network from offshore under infrastructure costing. Few people are working from offshore also. And their PCs or Laptops are being given by the vendor at offshore by charging to the customer.

At the same time the vendor might have considered the internal network team also to be billed at weekly few hours, because of their committed support for the customer hosted infrastructure at the premises.

Assuming these categories of the costing also budgeted by the IT Managers to the customer under SLAs.

Apart from the human resources costing with full time or part time, the infrastructure cost also need to be raised to the customer by the accounting team. If the automated systems are available the accounting tracking for all kinds of account heads will be easy with reference to the charging methods. This way one can feel the criticality of the automation of these processes for the IT Company.

Chapter Nine: The Dos and Don'ts for financial management

1.   The IT financial management teams should interact with several departments to understand the current and future costs for different activities while providing IT services to the internal and external customers.

2.   The underpinning contracts should be reviewed periodically to estimate the current and future cost of a service or a product.

3.   The maintenance cost of the equipments and their usage need to be tracked. The unused equipments maintenance contracts should be terminated in line with the relevant users.

4.   There should be strict cost control on costing as defined in the company's finance management policies.

5.   They should not allow the expenses as unapproved or those are beyond the policies.

6.   The finance team needs to have always a policing job to review and track the expenses occurring on different services, and should be measured against to the allocated or approved budget only.

7.   They also need to educate the relevant teams on the latest finance management policies of the company. So that there will not be self-esteem kind of clashes between the service management team and the finance team.

8.   The finance team needs to think they are the backbone of safeguarding the company's pennies and it is their role also.

Chapter Ten: The required Solutions and best practices

With all the above questions and from the examples discussed in different chapters; one can understand there is a need to have structured financial management practices in place within the company to sustain their business.

The ITIL [Information Technology Infrastructure Library] Life cycle supports for IT services building and executing with improvements. The IT startups need to follow these best practices incrementally. ITIL V3 provides the support for implementing the financial management process also.

In this E-Book I would like to elaborate on the required content from the ITIL best practices.

Following figure shows the five major phases of ITIL V3 Life Cycle.

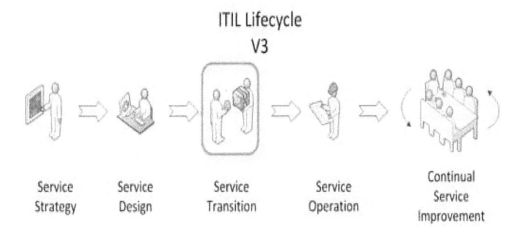

Figure 8: Five Phases of ITIL V3 Managed Across Life Cycle [MALC]

The financial management function is part of the IT Service Strategy [SS]. It is a core life cycle of IT service management [ITSM]. During the Service Strategy phase the IT Company need to define their services for their customers either with the customer's prior requirements or as new services introduction from the company. During this phase definition the services costing also need to be measured for their investment plans. So the prior budgeting can be done for those services costing.

Following Figure denotes the Service Strategy [SS] integrated processes:

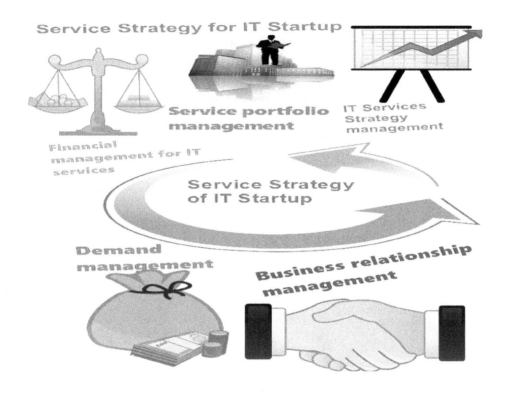

Figure 9: ITIL V3 Service Strategy integrated processes usage

Now as per the agenda of this E-Book content, let us restrict to the financial management topic only within the Service Strategy of ITIL practices. The below chapter can elaborate on these sub-processes.

Chapter Eleven: What are the sub-processes of financial management

The financial management has the below sub-processes as per the ITIL V3 Service Strategy practices:

- Financial management support

- Financial planning

- Financial analysis and reporting

- Service invoicing

- Business case

The below figures depicts these sub-processes integration:

Sub-processes of financial management

Figure 10: ITIL V3 Service strategy integrated sub-processes of financial management

Financial management support: It defines the required structures for the management in preparing the financial planning data and costs. It also illustrates the allocation of costs to different services. A periodical tracking mechanism will be applied from this support activity. You can refer to the accounting support also.

Example/Scenario:

Recollect the examples mentioned on invoicing process. The finance team support adds value at the point for billing and evaluating the costing also.

Financial planning: Using this process it can be determined the required financial resources during the next budget planning period. And it can allocate the resources for optimum benefits. When the vendor [IT Company] defined the services for the customers the required budget planning can come into this sub-process. The IT manager's role is crucial along with the account managers for budgeting.

Example/Scenario:

As mentioned in the previous examples; for any new services or upgraded services the financial planning need to be there. This planning makes the management to estimate the required budget by having different planned activities.

Financial analysis and reporting: This process can support in analyzing the structure of service provisioning cost and the profitability of the services. The financial analysis allows the service portfolio management to make their informed decisions, when they decide to implement the changes to the service portfolio. It involves, the services predicted costing. Using this practice the estimated Profit [P] and Loss [L] measurement also can be forecasted.

Example/Scenario:

In any project or programme; for all the identified activities the budget is planned and allocated. During this budget planning a financial analysis is done to arrive into estimated budget.

While reporting; using the past financial analysis on different resources costing can help for regular reviews to have the better cost control.

Service invoicing: Every service will have the periodical [fortnight or monthly] invoicing to the customers. This process involves the invoicing on the provisioning of the services and transmission of the invoice to the customer.

Example/Scenario:

With reference to the Charging process; the invoicing is mandatory as mentioned in the previous examples.

The importance of a Business case: Please note every financial requirement or a proposal needs a business case. Using business case everybody in the organization can understand easily on the proposed spending. The accountant needs to keep tracking for these business cases on every budgeting area.

Example/Scenario:

In any Project or Programme management; the business case is mandatory.

The business case justifies with the below questions:

Why should we do this project?

Who are going to benefit?

What savings or ROI can be arrived after this project completion?

Let consider any of the examples mentioned in the previous chapters. All of them should have the defined business case. Through the business case only the budgeting can be planned. The Finance team verifies the costing from the norms mentioned in the business case also. Hence without business case there is no project exists. Even any Project Management methodology insists for business case as mandatory.

Chapter Twelve: The importance of the Enterprise Architecture in place

In this chapter we can evaluate different situations of a Company and the best practices.

As per the ITIL definition: The financial management function and the processes are responsible for managing an IT service provider's; budgeting, accounting and charging requirements. Financial management for IT services secures an appropriate level of funding to design, develop, and deliver services that meet the strategy of the organization in a cost effective manner.

Hence through these best practices one can try to simulate for their organization to implement and achieve the high ROI. The following sections continue with the best practices along with some of the IT services live examples.

Example/Scenario:

The financial management function ensures any solution projected by IT services is to meet the requirements defined in service level management [SLM]; it is justified in view of its costing, budgeting and funding. The financial data should provide the cost associated with the changes in the IT infrastructure, systems, staffing and processes.

Let us assume the business is required with 100 human resources for a new Service providing with a new technology implementation. Then the IT financial management function should be able to provide all the costs involved in view of software, hardware, licensing and the ISP cost along with the human resources costing.

There can be different situation in a company depends on their internal setup or organization. Hence there can be adequate or inadequate financial management process might have been established earlier. Let us see those situations from the below sections.

What are the scenarios for inadequate and adequate financial management?

Let us assume a scenario; the startup company wants to implement the automation of the following:

- Incident management,
- Asset management,
- Help desk management,
- Accounting,
- Payroll
- HR process.

To complete these applications, we need to have:

a) People,

b) Software,

c) Hardware and

d) Support from the management.

The below figure can denote the scenario mentioned.

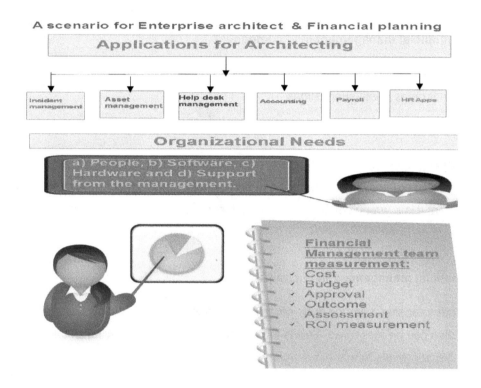

A scenario for Enterprise architect & Financial planning

Applications for Architecting

| Incident management | Asset management | Help desk management | Accounting | Payroll | HR Apps |

Organizational Needs

a) People, b) Software, c) Hardware and d) Support from the management.

Financial Management team measurement:
- Cost
- Budget
- Approval
- Outcome Assessment
- ROI measurement

Figure 11: Enterprise Applications Architecture for financial planning

The financial management team needs to measure their cost and budget them for approval. And at the same time they need to project the outcome. The reasonable profits or cost savings by using these applications can be measured with great returns.

Without financial management in IT company:

In this situation; there wouldn't be budgets. Everybody feels it costs the company when somebody denotes some suggestions.

Example/Scenario:

We can recollect the previous chapters examples/scenarios for different projects estimation. Without knowing their costing nobody would start it. Hence without financial management it is a wrong concept for their business planning and execution.

With Financial management in IT company:

The budget forecasting can be done on any new proposal. The costs involved in it and the ROI also can be measured. This is a matured process step by having all these in place to get approvals from the management.

Example/Scenario:

By having all these practices in place they are in track for measuring the ROI. The previous examples in different chapter would work correctly for cost control and to gain the better returns.

What is the scope of IT Financial management?

The financial management function is a well-known activity in any organization. It is imperative to understand the strategic approach that is adopted in relation to IT service provision in a startup IT Company.

Example/Scenario: In most of the IT startup companies they run behind the customers to get the

Projects as a 1st priority. But when the customer is delaying the invoices payments they realize the value of managing funding related to the IT services. It denotes by having the lack of financial management practices and the company can go into loosing further projects, skilled and experienced resources, and non-payment of bills on time, etc...

Eventually, it can create havoc in their business sustainability or continuation of the company stand. On my global experiences I have seen, top 20% of the customers only pay the bills on time. Hence you need to put the clause in SLA under provider terms & conditions as the invoice should be paid within a week of completion of 30 days or two weeks serviced cycle. You need to opt for the billing cycle. This can mitigate the risk of delaying the invoice payments. The customer can agree or sometimes they prefer to have that clarity in SLA. This way it can protect the company's business continuation.

Chapter Thirteen: Best practices for financial operations and internal strategy

With reference to the above chapters in this E-Book, it is well known to have the financial operation as mandatory for any startup IT Company to safeguard their business and its continuity. The below scenario elaborates on following the best practices.

Example/Scenario: In most of the large IT organizations, there are qualified accountants as in-charge of corporate finances. And they will be part of the finance department. They will have capabilities in setting up the financial policies, standards, and accounting practices for the business.

When the new or updated services are introduced with their defined practices they will be able to come up with the budgeting and the ROI. And the funding strategy will be the overall part of their accounting practices and approach. The specifics of the services can be managed by the demand manager, Business Relationship manager, steering committee, etc. roles locally.

Hence the team engaged in financial management of IT services should ensure the accounting practices are followed consistently with the existing corporate controls. The relevant reporting and accounting activities meet with the governance standards as defined for the whole organization. This practice also can support the various units in understanding on IT funding process. It can create the environment or culture to own responsibility on introducing the IT services with reduced cost and reasonable ROI to any unit.

By using the service level management approach, one can get an idea and responsibility to deliver the services by understanding 'the accounting for IT services is more effective, detailed, and efficient'.

Chapter Fourteen: Talent acquisition and retention management

In the current competitive global market, talent and the retention management is a major challenge to any small or midsized company.

Since this book talks on cost control; I wrote this section to cove the following contents for a mid or small sized IT services company to function cost effectively by using some of the below practices.

Every IT services company need to maintain the resources retention management. This section is not only useful for HR teams and also to the heads of the talent management groups, HR Policy makers, Delivery teams, Sales/marketing teams, etc... who all are responsible for resources retention and grooming within the organization to demonstrate the resource costing effectively and efficiently on a quarterly basis with the accelerated ROI.

The talent acquisition and management involves the different activities. Those are mentioned through the below chart:

Talent acquisition and management

Skills assessment	Orient on talent need	Form special hiring group

Competency building	Typical process steps involved	Involve Customer

Identify talent		Recruitment

Assess talent

Figure 12: Talent Acquisition and management

By observing the above process steps or activities, below questions might arise in our mind:

- ➢ What is skills assessment?

- ➢ What is competency?

- ➢ What is Talent?

- ➢ What is talent Acquisition?

- ➢ What is the role of recruitment team?

- ➢ The Talent acquisition needs to go through with whom?

- ➢ What are the steps need to be adopted for talent acquisition?

- ➢ What are the steps to follow after talented professionals are acquired?

Now, through the below sub-sections all the activities have been addressed.

What is special skills assessment?

Any resource has a specific role to play within an organization. That role needs specific duties and responsibilities to be performed by the resource. To drive the resource to perform the role effectively and efficiently some special parameters need to be applied through past experiences gained and some of the past lessons learnt also within the organization.

These special parameters can be called as skills of a resource. These skills need to be built by the resource incrementally or by attending special trainings. After attending the trainings the resource need to apply his/her thought on how to use them for the job role. Sometimes the role needs to be performed competitively against to the other vendor resource of a customer to grab the business deals or towards the business continuity of a business critical customer.

What is competency?

In normal or average performance situation the resources need not think about the competency. If a resource need to perform the role competitively, the skills need to be groomed to accelerate the performance. If the performance acceleration is driven well by the management or the organization, then the resources can be listed in the top performers team or group. This group is called high performance teams or groups or star performers within the organization.

The competencies need to be accelerated to sustain these groups. Ultimately, these groups can become as Talent group for an organization. In every organization atleast, top 15-30% of the resources belong to these categories to sustain the organization's global presence and also to compete with the other vendor's in-front of their strategic customers by demonstrating their importance and need in their account.

Then the meaning for BCP [Business continuity plan] can be successful for an organization. Otherwise, overnight they need to run behind the global market for a competent resources hiring with high paid cost, in turn it can generate the negative ROI also for a company, which is a bad management practice for returns.

What is Talent?

If any resource has developed the skills and demonstrated the performance as star performer or competent performer he or she can be considered as talented resource. To become a talented resource one need to accelerate the competencies and demonstrate them on different projects or programs in an organization.

What is talent Acquisition?

Most of the times, the Talented people will not be available right away in the market. The organization need to consider the competent people and groom them into a talent pool. Once they are in the talent pool they can be utilized for any kind of code red projects or major risk based projects to streamline them as a formula for a BCP of a specific customer account.

What is the role of recruitment team?

In any organization a typical recruitment team needs to perform their activities against to the existing positions fulfillment only. The existing positions cannot consist the role for competent or talented resource requirements. To recruit these talent positions a separate team need to be established with a special focus to understand the roles very clearly and to catch the right resource for the organization's burning issues resolution from the market.

At the same time this category of hiring team need to be groomed on interviewing skills also to catch the right resource in the market.

Talent acquisition needs to go through with whom?

The talent acquisition needs to go through with a talent hiring group, not with the regular recruitment team. The team of this group, responsibilities is to understand the organization's burning issues deeply. And define the needs of the talent resource requirements. They are also responsible to identify the sources of these resources availability. The relevant techniques need to be developed and applied to grab such resources faster onto the board to complete the internal prioritized activities for their deployment on the engagements.

What are the steps need to be adopted for talent acquisition?

The talent acquires group need to identify the organization's burning issues. They need to study the root causes. They need to conduct a gap analysis on these issues. Identify the resolutions or remedy. Then define the new talent resource requirements. Study the market to get the information on these resources availability at different global locations. Plan to have connection with them.

Educate on the organization's vision and goals to the talent people. Then explain the current needs and their contribution importance in the organization. Negotiate with their expectations. Demonstrate the organization's flexibility and make the environment professional way. Till they join keep them in connection with personal meetings by boosting the organization's latest trends, growth and achievements. Create the image as there is no such opportunity to the candidate except joining in this company for their career acceleration. With this practice understanding one can estimate what level of recruitment skills are required to acquire these resources.

What are the steps to follow after talented professionals are acquired?

Once the talent professional joined, they need to be in orientation program. During this program the entire organization history need to be presented along with the necessary improvements made timely to boost it to the market. The Year by Year business growth also needs to be discussed along with the achievements in those years. This makes their mindset to stick on to the company.

Once the orientation program is done, their feedback need to be assessed. It needs to be passed to the relevant position hiring department. This department needs to understand the sense of the new talent professional and accordingly it should be handled.

Few of the organizations might be practicing the legacy practices that need to be upgraded as per the latest trends also as practice of resource retention. Please collect the past quarterly results of the companies. They publish the cost involved in resources hiring also at the same time they publish the attrition % also QTR by QTR.

The newly hired talent professional need to attend the role based training also with the relevant project or program team. With this session, the new resource can understand the role and the need of hiring him/her. Ultimately, the questions can be posed during the session by the trainers to get the feeling of his/her views on these issues. The required resolutions need to be implemented can be discussed.

This practice can make the delivery team feel easy, not only in assessing the new resource talents and also the solutions where he/she can provide to the customers towards accelerating the CSAT. Once the role based training is completed, another talented professional or senior person within the organization needs to handle and engage this new resource, till the resource feels comfortably.

This resource retention techniques need to be applied in a constant and continuous basis. If at all any ignorance is made within the organization, he/she can fly away from the organization. Then the talent hiring wheel needs to be re-started with heavy efforts and cost to the company. Where it can generate the negative ROI.

In this chapter, I would like to bring into the notice of the global business leaders on the practices of hiring and firing activity. Most of the times these happens to the well performed resources also due to some of their internal situations.

Globally, the employee hiring and firing became as one of the companies HR practices since decades. Even if the resources are being well performed, these practices are being continued for meeting their ad-hoc or lack of long term strategy business plans or practices with their sudden cost cutting measures.

And after one or two months they will be running behind the market to hire the same kind of profiles by paying 20-30% [measured as lowest hikes], or for some roles even 60-80% hikes can happen to meet the revenue targets faster.

These practices can be a kind of passion or business ethics for large or globally established companies when they are earning billions or trillions of dollars under profits acceleration practices. These practices can happen without doing their internal maths on the resources cost benefit analysis. But the IT Startups or small sized companies cannot follow the large companies practices by burning their fingers.

- Then, what happens to the IT Startup company resource retention practices in this case?
- How the resources can be adjusted in the company?
- What are the ways the startups should utilize the resources?
- What are the cost and benefit analysis with the existing resources a company can look into?
- What kind of profits and advantages they can get by retaining the well performed resources?
- How they can measure the resources bench period costing?
- How long they can be maintained in bench with profits?
- What will be their new skills training costs?
- What are the performance differences between existing and newly hired resources?
- Do you count the resources learning duration?
- Do you feel the new resource will give the same productivity from day one?

We can see most of the answers from this section with a cost benefit analysis and Tables given below by examples. It can help in better planning or best resource management practices implementation.

Table-1:

IT Billable Resources retention Profit and Loss analysis	Resource A	Resource B	Resource C
Experience in Years	3	6	10
Role	Developer	Designer	PM
Skills			
Hourly Billing Rate [in Indian Rupees]	1,000 INR	1,300 INR	1,500 INR
Monthly Revenue [in Indian Rupees]@160hrs	160,000 INR	208,000 INR	240,000 INR
Monthly CTC [in Indian Rupees]	50,000 INR	70,000 INR	100,000 INR
Monthly Proffit by Resource	110,000 INR	138,000 INR	140,000 INR
Yearly Revenue	1,920,000 INR	2,496,000 INR	2,880,000 INR
Yearly CTC	600,000 INR	840,000 INR	1,200,000 INR
Yearly Profit by resource	1,320,000 INR	1,656,000 INR	1,680,000 INR
Yearly Profit % by resource	220 INR	197 INR	140 INR
Resource productivity increase in % after one year	175	150	130
Aditional benefit to company in revenues by month	50000.75	70000.75	100000.75
After one year of resource billing profit analysis [Let us Assume, the resource was on one year project with continuous billing. Suddenly the client terminated the project. Then assuming you want to keep 50% of the resource profit with company and still how many months you can bear the resource on bench.]			

Table1 shows the existing billable resources Profit and Loss analysis, with one year service of the resource with continuous billing.

Below Table2 shows the benefits of keeping them on bench with their training plans/costs and the duration of bench period.

Table2:

Role	Developer	Designer	PM
Number of months credit for bench	26	24	17
After taking away 50% profit	13	12	8
Training duration of the resource for new skills [Let us say you invest two months of resource salary for one month of intensive training. But still after training also you keep the resource on bench]	1	1	1
Number of months on bench	12	11	7
If you fire the resource after project termination			
Hire for new project [in every new project, you will have to pay 20-30% higher than the existing resources.]			
Cost analysis With new resources augmentatio			
Experience in Years	3	6	10
Role	Developer	Designer	PM
Skills			
Hourly Billing Rate [in Indian Rupees]	1,000 INR	1,300 INR	1,500 INR
Monthly Revenue [in Indian Rupees]@160hrs	160,000 INR	208,000 INR	240,000 INR
Monthly CTC [in Indian Rupees]	60,000 INR	84,000 INR	120,000 INR
Profile/candidate supply cost [one month salary]	60,000 INR	84,000 INR	120,000 INR
Internal hiring cost [1.5 Months CTC]	60,000 INR	84,000 INR	120,000 INR
Total Expenses after upto hiring	120,000 INR	168,000 INR	240,000 INR
Monthly Proffit by Resource	100,000 INR	124,000 INR	120,000 INR
Yearly Revenue	1,920,000 INR	2,496,000 INR	2,880,000 INR
Yearly CTC	720,000 INR	1,008,000 INR	1,440,000 INR
Yearly Profit by resource	1,200,000 INR	1,488,000 INR	1,440,000 INR
Monthly Loss or difference by having new resource	10000	14000	20000
Yearly Loss or difference by having new resource	120000	168000	240000
New resource Productivity loss in % by role	30	40	60
Your CSAT rating reduction in points [out of 5]	2.5	2	1.5

Table3:

After one year	Developer	Designer	PM
Productivity	175.00 %	150.00%	130.60%
	Developer	Designer	PM
Yearly Profit % by resource	220	197	140

Profit by resource in %

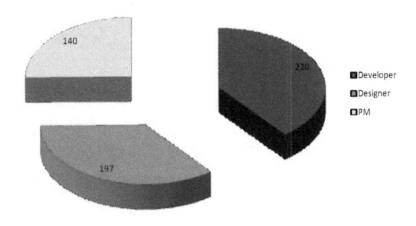

Table3 shows the Profit and loss analysis on the new resources after the one year serviced resources were fired.

Table4:

New Resource loss			
	Developer	**Designer**	**PM**
Productivity	-30.00%	-40.00%	-60.00%

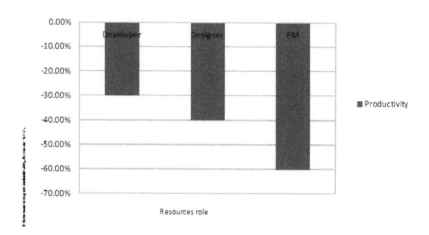

Loss by new resources

We can observe from **Table4**, Always the new resources learning time and mixing up takes some time to meet the company and customer demands.

After doing all the above maths, one can decide on the resources strategy depends on their internal status or their current business plans.

Above questions have been addressed by this Profit [P] and Loss [L] Analysis.

Conclusion:

Hope from this E-Book if the readers belong to IT Services Company and who holds the responsibility of managing the services, they can streamline their current processes towards their accelerated ROI. Please leave your comment if you feel others can use it.

Please feel free to contact me. My blog site has my contact details.

Shanthi Kumar Vemulapalli is a seasoned professional with 25+ years of global IT experience in cost-effectively utilizing technology in alignment with corporate goals. Delivered bottom-line ITSM results through competent project and program management solutions, successful development and execution of systems, and implementation of best practices.

Recognized for inculcating a culture of innovation and knowledge sharing in organizations. Built teams for many companies globally; through training, mentoring and guiding the IT resources along with the on project competencies building. Supported for many infrastructure setups and conversion related projects [onsite/offshore model].

His Professional Certifications: ITIL V3 Expert Certification – Service Lifecycle, PRINCE2 Practitioner Certification, Lean Six Sigma Black Belt, Cloud computing Foundation [EXIN] and Certified Tester Foundation Level [CTFL].

He also wrote several blogs on the IT related topics. They are available in the below sites:

1. http://vskumarblogs.wordpress.com/

2. http://vskumarcloudblogs.wordpress.com/

3. http://vskumar35.wordpress.com/

Other publications: by Shanthi Vemulapalli

Please view the below link for the author's published E-books on different topics:

http://www.amazon.com/s/ref=dp_byline_sr_ebooks_1?ie=UTF8&text=Shanthi+Vemulapalli&search-alias=digital-text&field-author=Shanthi+Vemulapalli&sort=relevancerank

www.ingramcontent.com/pod-product-compliance
Lightning Source LLC
Chambersburg PA
CBHW070859070326
40690CB00009B/1913